HERE'S LOOKING AT YOU KID

Helen Burke was born in Doncaster, 1953, and started writing poetry in the 1970s. Since then she has amassed an impressive record of competition victories, including the Manchester International, the Suffolk Poetry Prize, and the Ilkley Literature Performance Poetry Prize (twice). Her work has been published in *Rialto, New Welsh Review, Northwords, Dreamcatcher*, as well as in numerous anthologies and pamphlets. Her first full-length collection, *The Ruby Slippers*, was published by Valley Press in 2011.

Here's Looking at You Kid

HELEN BURKE

Valley Press

First published in 2014 by Valley Press
Woodend, The Crescent, Scarborough, YO11 2PW
www.valleypressuk.com

First edition, first printing (August 2014)

ISBN 978-1-908853-42-4
Cat. no. VP0057

Printed and bound in Great Britain by
Imprint Digital, Upton Pyne, Exeter

www.valleypressuk.com/authors/helenburke

Contents

Introduction   7

Here's Looking at You Kid   11
Dad's Lingo   12
The Kids with the Tree House   14
Hospital Lingo   15
French Cat in French Window   17
The Serving Girl   18
The Old Pig   20
My Wild Mother   23
The Kindness Medal   25
The Christmas Letter   26
Eight o'clock in Britain   28
All You Need is Love   30
Sixties Anthem   33
Baxter's Crime   34
The Kindness of Dogs   36
Distance   38
A wheelchair goes into a bar   39
The Open Door   41
The Lucky Dip Machine of the Magic Bird of
   Fortune   42
My Mother, the Mustang   44
What They Found in the Poet's Stomach   46
Keats in Piazza Navona   47
Watcher of the Skies   48
The Romany Ghosts of My Father   49
The Green Piano   53
Starting Over   54

Notes   57

Introduction

And you ask me, why I continue to write? And I guess I would have to say, it's like climbing a mountain –

It's just what I do – I keep on writing. It's what brings me back my soul and keeps me sane.

Writing is what keeps me singing in the rain.

Walking back from mass as a kid, in the snow, with my mum, we used to look at all the different footprints – people, dogs, cats, birds – and wonder who they were and where they were going. 'What journey are they on?' I used to ask her.

My mother, being who she was, probably had a good idea – although I don't recall she ever told me.

I never know where I'm going with a poem. Often I just take it on trust that the words know best and that I too am leaving my own footprints in the snow, for those reading and walking back home to wonder about. Companions in the blizzard, maybe?

Here's Looking at You Kid is a new collection of poems, but with an emphasis on poems people often specifically ask me to perform – perhaps because at that moment on that particular day, it seemed relevant to something in their own lives, and reminded them of their own footprints.

Every flake of snow has its own unique pattern and I hope that each of the poems is like that. My dad loved to watch Humphrey Bogart films and that's how this book got its title – 'here's looking at you, kid' was a kind of code between us.

I like to think that Dad and Louis are still walking off into the distance – and going to put right all the injustices of the world. You have to have a dream as the snow falls, and that's one of mine.

Poems that people ask for are either dogs playing in the snow or strange white snowmen come to life, or they are

Narnia and it is never ever Christmas, or they are great white snowbirds flying and wheeling and diving up high in the sky.

Some of these poems have been requested for weddings, some for anniversaries, some for funerals, and some for landmark birthdays. So this collection focuses on poems that people have felt they could relate to in a very personal way.

Also in this collection I am very proud to say I have the winning poem for last year's Torbay Poetry Competition, which was a delight when I received the news. There are also a number of poems which were written specifically for the Keats-Shelley House in Rome in this Keats anniversary year. It was a privilege to judge the Young People's Poetry Prize there, as well as perform in the house.

Poems are, for me, a way of riding the carousel horse clean off the carousel. Magical? I hope so. Someone said to me last night at a poetry reading that it was one of the first poetry events they had been to, and that they had connected with the poems at a heart level, as a human being. I felt quite proud of continuing to write at that moment.

I hope that these poems can connect with you at a heart level also – and that they bring you joy, laughter, and a little of that carousel magic.

Helen Burke

Here's Looking at You Kid

Here's Looking at You Kid

I noticed from an early age that the sun
asked permission to be on our street.
'Is the sun allowed here?' I once asked me dad,
and even though he knew it wasn't
he pulled his collar high and looked all round –
then put it in his pocket just for me.
Even though he knew to own this bright,
this dangerous thing would bring me
perils, as well as joy.
(Better to have a little sun than none at all.)

And we walked home, like two happy dogs
and the sky was duck-egg blue and the grass
was full of four-leaved clovers
and Dad winked – and we laughed to think
he had the sun in his pocket.

'Here's looking at you, kid,' Dad said.
'Here's looking at you.'

Dad's Lingo

You ask me what his lingo was
and the only way I can explain is this:
the Irish for yes – is no
and the Irish for no – is yes.
If he said he liked someone, that meant that he only
    tolerably
hated them.
If he said he couldn't stand them,
at any price nor be in the same room even –
this meant he had definitely warmed to them,
would be prepared to have a drink with them. Give them
    the benefit
of some soldierly, hard-won advice. Oh, yes.
If he said he would do a thing directly – this meant you
    could wave it bye-bye.
Permanento.
As much chance as a female pope. As likely as him selling
    his Mario Lanza LPs.
If he said he could not, *would* not be persuaded, no, not even
    if a glass of Guinness
stood between the thing and himself – you could guarantee
    success within the
hour.
Sooner, quicker than a gnat's dream. As certain as a plenary
    indulgence.
This was my father's lingo.
And to say I understood it – does not do him justice. Part of
    the time I understood part of him
and all of the time I understood none of him – although
    some of the time he allowed me

to think that I had followed the circuitous path of his
extraordinary thinking. Oh, yes.

And the rest of the time – he translated what he could.
Myself, the poor eejut.

He allowed me to believe that I had made sense of his
words.

But behind my back – I knew he was laughing. (And I am
so glad he was.)

The Irish for yes is – no

and the Irish for no – is yes.

The Kids with the Tree House

How we hated them.
Then. The unthinkable – they asked us to tea.
Me and our lad.
So, we went.
Trudged up to the Big House, walked on the gravel
(what the hell's that?) Mummy showed us the way.
The garden – jeez – the size of the park
and them sitting up in their lofty domain.
You watched as they climbed the ladder, high into the leafy
green world. All luscious and beckoning.
We followed. Drank from the acorn cups,
ate off the bamboo plates. Little May had brought Teddy up.
You held him to ransom, by his leg right over the edge.
You kicked the ladder away as we scrambled off.
The boy tried to be brave, but May screamed and screamed.
They were no match for you – with their acorn agenda and
    gravel
stupendous. We ran, all the way home.
And you had egg and chips, and went out with the bad lads
from the dodgy end of the street.
And I couldn't eat mine – kept seeing May's face.
And Mam said – 'How was it? Tea with the posh lot?'
And I said – 'Can we have a tree house?'
And Mam said – 'There's the park down the road. How
    many
trees do you bloody want?'

Hospital Lingo

There's a lot of it about
in here.
It starts with 'the procedure', which will be
carried out whether I like it or not. Makes no odds – you can be
watching *Deal or No Deal* – and they'll still do it.
It will be done with a bicycle pump and a packet of Caramac.
Then a pair of tweezers – and I'll be smeared all over with
a sausage roll. It's for me own good.
Chrissie at the end is having everything removed,
piece by piece – her sanity, her sense of humour, her husband.
She's quite glad about the last.
Another poor sod is having all her bits sewn back on, but this time
in the right order. (The spleen is such an undecorative item.)
And the bag it came in – hers to keep, if she wants. There's thoughtful.
We have all been here longer than we would like.
Our visitors – poor limping specimens – come in just to cheer
themselves up. They are free to leave – cocky beggars.
We compare.
I've had mine scraped and flagellated and crimped. Then run up a flagpole. And still
it works with all the good grace of a banjo with no strings.
Maureen has had a pipe put down and a frog inserted where the blue dye spilled out. The frog is none too happy, either.

Cynthia – bless – has had it all twirled around and blown
   up, so all the first-year students could get
a really good look – then she was rinsed and parboiled and a
hollandaise mouse was frozen in a time capsule and buried
   in her
second-best handbag. (Like on *Masterchef*.)
The woman who used to be a vicar – has been Emanuelled
   and
had the tattoo of Cliff Richard finally removed. She had a
   vision in the night of Bjorn from Abba giving her the kiss
   of life. Which is a worry.
And the little lass in the side room (sectioned) keeps *on*
   singing –
'We'll meet again Kathleen' – then running naked down to
   the front doors.Why wouldn't she – she's been Nil By Life
   since she was born.
Anyway – it's an ill wind – because –
they come in later to tell me that it's all going on nicely.
Just the inner tube to remove in the morning from me arse,
and the orang-utan to strap to me chest, and the whistling
   giraffe to come up with me tablets, and I can go.
Still, they do a lovely bit of fish – on a Friday.
If only it were Friday.
Is it Friday?
Is it?

French Cat in French Window

So. I am a French cat in a French window and you
are just passing by – you take my photograph –
why wouldn't you? – because I am beautiful.
I am beautiful – and you are English – that's how the cookie
    crumbles – yes, life can be unfair. Life can be a dog.
I am licking my arse – and I am still beautiful – don't try
it yourself. I can't be responsible for hospital bills.
I am a French cat in a French window – you are on your
way to – how you say it – Yorkshire?
I am on my way to Montmartre to buy a little sardine
on a bed of couscous – perhaps a little wine, if the year
she seems a good one. You look very pale – as if
your whole world, she is not coloured in and has no
way of turning the other cheek – and looking up at the moon
and singing in the night. At midnight.
That is when the French cat comes to life.
I myself run a little café in the Bois de Boulogne. I even
let a few English sit at the tables there. But, at this moment
I am cleaning my bottom – with the care of an artiste –
and you take my photograph.
I feel a little sorry for you – but even so, as you click your
    camera
I will turn my arse right around to face you.
This is – how you call it? –
the French Resistance.

The Serving Girl

Though I never knew her
I bear her name.
Margareta. My grandmother.
She is undismissable.
Sitting at the sea's edge,
a moon-faced dog at her side.
Eyes – neat as jet.
Skin the colour of turtle doves.
The lick of salt in her hair,
dark with time.

Here, next to her, is a blue pot that mutters.
Let us call it, the sea.
It contains all the words we never spoke.
It is held in our four hands
that never touched.
Fierce as flint, the years that lie between us.
Plaiting and unplaiting the dark memory
of your hair.
Though I never knew you, I bear your name.

I imagine the stairs you climbed in the grand house.
The starched minute hand of the clock
ticking in the hall.
The mistress of the house checking your apron.
Your presence in your own absence.
Nothing to be done but bear it.
I imagine the meals on silver trays carried back and
    forth.
The perfectly folded white cloths.
All with initials. None of them yours.

I can almost smell the blooms of white clematis
as it hung near your window.
In winter they will cut it back, and you will miss it so.

Did the house have a hundred rooms? I want to ask.
And was yours the finest Margareta?
Your secret name that lies on cloth invisible,
that now must serve for memory.
Only her voice, that is the salt, that is the sea,
answers me.

I swill her voice around my empty head.
I watch the tide that cannot call her home.
A prism of water in my throat. My throat that
glinting, swells, becomes the sea.
A final call that earths two names. A shaft of sunlight.
Our meeting now – like this. Incredible.
The pure chance of her wave ending
right where mine began.

The Old Pig

He was old, you told me.
The pig I now imagine, hanging sweet as a bag of sugar out
    in the barn.
Your job was always to feed him – and him
licking your hand as if it were pressed silk.
So many times, you told me the story.
Your guts turning, churning – knowing his future.
Brushing the long crease of your skirt –
watching him eat. Fat, contented.
Turning the iron handle of the sty door –
a kind jailer you must have seemed.
The sky above the door – blue as your eyes.
And the straw in his heart – stiff with fright on that last
    day.
Both of you willing that day not to come, but knowing it
    would.
Your face turned away to the sky –
love and anguish mixed with mud – a bloody cocktail.
Every ambush requires that there are two.
Your hand on the door, closing it.
The old pig, listening for your voice, found only silence.
Turn his face to the sky, you tell the men.
You replay the ambush many times through all the years.
Because the pig forgives you.
Endlessly.
Even as they bring the knife towards him.
He forgives you.

My Wild Mother

My mother's at that difficult age
between 81 and 81-and-a-half.
She says she's not a senior citizen,
just a citizen.
She plays hookey from church bazaars,
borrows my kitten mules and feather boa
and hangs round bars in town.
Wears gold studs through her false teeth.
Has had a Lancaster bomber
tattooed on her left arm.
(We won't talk about her right.)
Men from the over-sixties club
leave things for her in the porch
in plain brown wrappers.
She says she's saving chat rooms
for the New Year. After Bruges.
When she's bored.
Did I mention Bruges?
There's been talk of Bruges for Christmas
with Hal, the American she met
at salsa class. (Sixty-four, all his own teeth.)
She's fitting him in between life-modelling for
the man who mends the boiler
and shamanic journeying to rid herself
of life's little obstacles.
(Me, apparently.)

She buys shop cakes recklessly, now she no longer bakes.
My father's allotment has become a figure of fun and she
was seen giving the last of its produce to the poor and
   needy
at the DSS. (That's the staff.)
I can't bring myself to ask why it has to be a lift
at the Co-op to scatter Dad's ashes.
She has been banned from the Countrywomen's Guild
for rap-dancing and spitting.
Her talk on voodoo – 'How it can improve your sex life' –
has been put on indefinite hold.

Everyone says there's no need to worry.
That they're all the same at that age. It's just their hormones
   running amok.
That it's just a phase we'll look back on and laugh.
The sign on her bedroom door still reads – 'Access denied
to those not from the Planet Zog.'
Apparently – if I want to keep her –
I'll have to let her go.
(It's all very complicated.)
All I know is – her Perry Como collection lies in pieces in
   the bin
and underneath her pillow, there's a one-way ticket.
   (Bruges).

The Kindness Medal

This is a medal for kind people.
It was minted in the
Can't-Be-Arsed-To-Be-Bothered-With-Them factory.
It will be ignored, not even brought out
on special occasions, like days that you breathe on, and
it will be stored in vaults, and knocked-down shacks
and will-o'-the-wisp caves and dust-riddled libraries that
no-one, not even Philip Larkin, ever goes in –
and it will be unsung about and unwritten about
and spiders will weave webs around it and its colour
will fade and the ribbon it would have hung from
will be lost and the little gold box it came in
will be broken and stood on and splintered
and no-one will know, or worse, care.
It will be unremembered in a thousand small ways
in every city in the glib and transient world.
This is the Medal of Honour, for Kind People
and it will never, ever, be given to them.

The Christmas Letter

Hallo.
This is just to let you know that
we're doing an awful lot
better than you.
Jessica got her PhD in
terminal snobbery
and Joshua hopes not to work, too.
We've got Mummy with us
still in the annexe –
you'd hardly know she was there,
except for the odd fallout of money
and last few bits of hair.

We've had ten holidays, all of them foreign,
and Jem's wedding at the Abbey was fab.
The Caribbean beckons for Christmas, again,
and my new facelift's arrived from the lab.
Life is going swimmingly. And we do –
swim, that is, whenever we can.
We've been walking in Tuscany, the Dordogne and Sidcup,
and we're friends of a friend of Cherie's old man.

All the kids have had nose jobs
and the cat's booked in for a boob job,
but the gardener's making do with reiki and several flu
    jabs.
My cocaine habit's coming on nicely
and the twins have made a blue movie – *so* hip.
Daddie's married our nanny – again – and
he'll be off to the Philippines
(once his heart can face the trip).

The dog has got his own Rolex
and the tax office can't smell a rat –
we trail our successes behind us
and the bank balance purrs like a cat.
We can't put a foot wrong. We've clawed our way up
through the school of soft knocks,
and that's that. We feel sorry for you
with your dope and your glue –
and your nose stud and weird rainbow hat.

We're doing so bloody, appallingly, awfully well –
don't you just hate us to absolute hell?

Eight o'clock in Britain

It's always eight o'clock in Britain.
No matter how you try and avoid it – it looms.
Like Groundhog Day.
It's always too late to *go* anywhere, *do* anything.

(Friend – it's too late not to do it, go there.)

In Barcelona, Paris, Rome they'll be promenading.
We walk round Huddersfield, Halifax, Hades and Hull –
we get the train to Doncatraz, across to York,
then down to Epping, Reading, Rhyl –
it's eight o'clock and the country has closed.
May as well be Knocking on Heaven's Door.
(Ever feel you've been here before?)
Its eight o'clock and growing late –
it's later than you think, mate.

Everywhere the same story.
Lights on in one kebab stop –
served by a yellow-eyed dog called Delaney,
the owner, asleep in the Back of the Shop.
Everyone's on drugs. *That* drug –
The 'Sod you. We're closed. Closed and you can piss off, pal'
      drug.
The 'Bog off abroad, if you're that bloody bothered.
We don't do promenades round here', mainline stuff.
Nah – we do the *Racing Times* and *Nuts* blowing round the
      city centre.
We do four lads in hoodies that look older than me dad
eating chips. And two lasses – pretending to be coquettish
      but really
only after t'chips.

Its eight o'clock and Britain has switched off, is in shutdown,
    meltdown, crackdown,
backdown, blowndown, growndown, thistledown,
eiderdown, walkaround
pissed town.
It's eight o'clock and get yourself indoors – because
we don't do promenades round here – if you want that sort
    of crap
piss off abroad. That's more your thing (you look the type).
It's eight o'clock and we've got glass slippers on our feet.
It's eight o'clock in Britain – and growing late.

Ain't that right?
It's later than you think, mate.

All You Need is Love

There is no 'of course' about love.
There is no boat you cannot land,
no truth you cannot understand,
there is no 'of course' about love.
There are no grey jagged rocks,
no only black and white –
only a hand reaching out to make it all alright,
out, out of the depths.
There is no barking dog to pass by,
only a stray cat with no tail –
and you stood by the door, wondering how best to explain
what you cannot explain.
There is no 'of course' about love.
There is no easy Cluedo explanation,
no hammer in the hall, Miss Scarlett,
no revolver in the library being the reason why
Professor Pigeon had to die –
there is no spike you can remove with simple tweezers from
    the heart –
there is no elephant in your eye,
no badgers living in your feet,
there is no definite way to assure the people that you'll
    meet
that there is no 'of course' about love. Oh, no.
There is no map of your future,
no guarantee of sunny days –
but no reason in the world from hopes and dreams
to look the other way.
There is always tomorrow, no matter where you are.

No matter how thin your spirit's stretched,
there is no happiness you cannot catch,
there is no bad day that lasts forever,
there is a better way to be if
we all shine a light, together. Because
all you need is love. Love is all you need.
There is no door too small,
no bar that can't be raised – because
all you need is love
of *course* you do –
you can't kid me, pal –
I see right through you.
I wish I didn't, but I do.
There is no 'of course' about love –
the sweet impossible saving ways of it –
the undeniable light-filled days of it –
the mysterious hopeful ways of it –
love is all you need –
love is all you need –
love is all *we* need.

Sixties Anthem

If I remember correctly
it was the summer we wore dahlias
in our hair from my uncle Ted's garden – he never knew
until years later that we were the culprits that scalped the
  earth. It was the summer that
we hitched a ride to Leeds and smoked dope with two truck
  drivers
until we were so stoned we pretended to be runaway trainee
  nuns
who the Pope was about to excommunicate because we had
  worn suspenders.
Visible suspenders. And then being dropped off at my aunt
  Chrissie's house
and her lying dead drunk on the floor from the beer affliction
and all and a man calling round with her new budgie and us
  taking it away with us
him not being keen on leaving it in the Guinness-dark
  parlour
where her head was wedged against the bathroom door.
Like an old dishcloth, you said.
Except her hair was red, I thought.
Like Scarlett O'Hara – a great wounded Scarlett O'Hara.
And us dangling the budgie over the edge of the Bar Walls
  where we believed
there was a better place for him to fly to, and the bird
  screaming and calling
out like there was no tomorrow.

But there always was a tomorrow. It was just
today and yesterday that were in doubt.
If I remember correctly.

Baxter's Crime

Baxter, the dog, is being dragged down the lane.
Again.
I feel sorry for Baxter, in fact, most days –
I feel a bit like him.
Pulled this way and that.
Someone behind me with a lead that I can't see.
Baxter has no idea what his crime is.
(Nor have I.)
Just that he is a dog who takes his time, perhaps.
He investigates. Sniffs too long in all the wrong places.
I can never hear the words – just that she is shouting,
snapping and snarling.
I imagine the teeth are bared – the hackles grizzly and
   raised.
But Baxter I feel is undeterred.
He will go on being Baxter.
He will go on going on.

There is no cure for being free of mind and will.
Baxter, my friend, my alter ego.
Baxter – I love you.
Go on being, Baxter.

(Run amok – remain a dog with pluck.)

You bark at your side of the wall
and I will bark at mine.

The Kindness of Dogs

You say it and it is true.
Dogs are kind.
They buy small dog treats for each other.
They hold doors open for cats.
They run rings around the moon,
bury the sun in the sand and throw sticks
for the stars.
Dogs are kind.
They put paws on your knees on bad days.
They hold a light out to you in their eyes.
They run to the top of the mountain and bark
'Which stone did you want? Which one?'
and race back down with it and place it gently at your feet.
Dogs are kind (you say it and it is true).
They bark in all the right places at the theatre and hide
behind the sofa in the scary movie. They share their ice
    cream
with you, no questions asked.
Our dog – Zorro – the one we have not met yet
will be our best chum, best in the whole world.
He will be faithful and strong.
In dreams he runs right up to me, barks and says:
'You look a little peaky, why not take a year off
and come with me to Zanzibar? Stretch your legs and chase
your tail. See all that world out there? It's yours for the
    asking.'
And he gives me one of his fleas as a token of goodwill.
Dogs are kind.
They run into the sea and look amazed that it is wet
but they do not take offence.

They love a through-breeze in their ears, hanging out of
   windows,
a breeze that says they're happy in all the different
   continents.
Dogs are good map-readers and they always
know a better route – past the poodle beauty parlour and
   turn
right at the Dog and Duck.
Dogs lay their heads beside you and know just what you're
   thinking.
Dogs' favourite word is walk.
Dogs are kind.

Distance

What is it? How should I call it?
This distance that holds not you –
rather you hold it.
Yet, if you were here, this distance
would be gone – as it is it has no colour
nor sound – only a memory of you.
In its shape you lie, an invisible inked
horizon.

The dust lies here too, as thick as thoughts,
like some foreign perfume,
impenetrable as the dreaming sea.
There is a new room between us –
it is a garland of possibilities. It grows
as you sleep. It judges I cannot reach you.
Each day more dust settles.
Each day in the new room, the pages are turning
in a book, by an open window, and there
a butterfly sits, its small pulse in the sun's light.
The music of all we said goes on.

for Dad, with thanks

A wheelchair goes into a bar

A wheelchair goes into a bar and
conversation stops
and people remember somewhere else they have to be like
Doncaster or Iraq –
a wheelchair goes into a bar
and voices are lowered because maybe
this is how them bastards caught the plague
just by being near *it* … a wheelchair
goes into a bar
and it's like a time traveller has come in –
one from the planet
'Fucking hell, wouldn't want to be them …'
and the air absents itself
and the flowers on the tables get removed
('cause, why would you?) – when
a wheelchair goes into a bar.

A wheelchair goes into a bar, right –
and everyone cares, but no-one looks
and there's obstacles called chairs
and people who will move
(preferably into another world)
and people who won't
and people who say
'I didn't know they came out at this time of night' –
and – 'That bloody man's caught my tights' –
oh yeah, a wheelchair goes into a bar.

A wheelchair goes into a bar
and if it's in Italy – people run out of the bar
and laugh, and carry you in and say you must be the Pope,

and if it's in France – people shrug their shoulders, cry,
tell you their life story and buy you cognac,
and if it's Ireland –
the bar is full of four hundred other wheelchairs each with
a stranger story than yours, so at least you feel ordinary –

and if it's Prague –
fifteen musicians, four monkeys and twelve art students
bring the bar *outside* to you.
Oh yeah. A wheelie goes into a bar.

A wheelchair goes into a bar
and just wants a bloody drink.

The Open Door

Stories are what make us who we are.
Stories are what make the blackbird sing, what make
a friend call by – what keep the open door ajar.
Stories are what get me through, what keep me
able to go on. (Some days, only just.)
So, my love – let's tell each other stories.
Stories make up 98% of my body – the other 2%
is chocolate mixed with hope.
A bird flies in through my open door – he tells me
he has word from you.
It seems you're doing okay – but you miss me.
In the bird's beak, you have sent a rose,
like those my father grew and those my mother loved –
the wildest roses from the lane.
I miss you too. I miss our story.
The one we told together every day.
You holding me – always my happy ending.
This bird is freedom and he beckons.
Come, he says, *let me take you to him – tell one last story.*
This small bird – how he suns himself by the open door.
No cage for him.
Freedom, only freedom in his eye and in his plumage.
The air, she smells of roses, and the crescendo of his flight.
My love, there is one last story, under the sun
and I am called to tell it now.
We are the stories that we tell not with our mouths but with
    our hearts.
Imagine. The beauty of it.
Flying with that bird.
Imagine.

The Lucky Dip Machine of the
Magic Bird of Fortune

And it reached out that long arm
at the fairground
into the shiny glass globe that was almost
as baffling and mysterious as the world itself –
and it reached out and into a shimmering, bobbling sea of
    blue teddy bears
and dogs with funny faces and sherbet dips and candyfloss
    key rings and star-
spangled clowns and angels with wands made of all my
    heart desired –
and found *you*.

And straight away – it knew what to do.

It defied gravity and sod's law (as well as a few others)
and it dipped down deep as if it was
hoping against hope and against all the odds
and because of all the reasons that things just don't work out
or that two people just miss each other by a second or two
    in the ether
and then they have to keep on going without each other
but always wondering and pretending
how life might have been –
and after a few near misses the silver arm came up for air

and with it there was *you*,

staring out at me from the other side of the glass world
and you looked as baffling and mysterious as the world
    itself.

(Who could wonder, with only the clowns to talk to…?)
And the lucky dip machine spoke and said –
'Take him home – this one here.'
And down you came – down the shiny glass chute
like magic, right into my arms.
And me, that never had much luck before, had to pinch
myself to see if it was true.
But the glass globe of mystery and the crazy bird of fortune
had spoken.
And the clowns waved you goodbye
and the angels flew.

My Mother, the Mustang

How it reminds me of you, that horse language.
That other being who stands at the far edge of the field.
Myself, seven heartbeats away – and you pawing at the
　　earth.
My mother, the mustang – the language of the mustang
a wild snatch upon the air.
In those last days, although you lay quietly
I know you saw everything as always, from the corner of
　　your eye
and – the lips moved slightly when I came into the room.
Sat by your bed – you said: '*I'm* alright, more to the point,
　　how are *you*?'
And then no answer, only a turning and a shifting of the
　　head, a soft brush
of the mane against my hand.
The language of the steppes was yours – the running wild,
　　the quiet grazing
and then the moving on. The wilderness calling you and
　　you so very glad
to go. You cannot tame a mustang.
Why would you even want to?

How it reminds me of you,
that other language that I never learnt to speak.
Only sitting by the bed, giving water to the lips,
bending low slowly to whisper in your ear, my love.
Thinking how fine the cheekbones that I've seen a million
　　times, and the hazel
Irish eyes – closed, but still they see me.

Breathing in through my stomach deeper and deeper
so that all your fears dissolve. The language of the mustang,
    always it was yours.
I watch you step softly, nearer to me – just one word to
    leave me with
before the moving on. That world you have longed for and
    dreamed of
where the spirit takes you to run free as free.
I see a group of your kin are gathering by the bed and with
    them
fear dissolves, and the breath in my body is almost gone
    with you.
The sound of your leaving, Mother, I know I will not hear –
just the sound of a river where it runs past the mountains
and the ground all around rich with hooves.

What They Found in the Poet's Stomach

What they found in the poet's stomach
was a dislike for bullshit on all levels.
A dislike for bullshit and a need to *declaim* that dislike.
They found a hatred of injustice and the gagging of
    freedom,
and the remains of several futile wars in the oesophagus.
It seems likely that they had drunk from the extremes
of poverty and calamity – and there was a residue of
famine and frailty in the bones – as if to know these
things would be to end them.
(Would that this were so…)
But mainly, overall – from Shelley to Keats, from Donne
to Dickinson to Plath to Byron and all the rest –
they found in the stomach lining itself – embedded in the
    gut –
the need for truth and the need for truth as beauty itself.
And this, without doubt, mi'lord
was the actual *cause* of death, of each and every poet
whose names are writ in water, stone and blood,
and still they write.

Keats in Piazza Navona

All life, all love, all laughter is here
in Piazza Navona
where the waiters look like film stars
and the film stars look like waiters, where the birds
in the trees have golden feathers and the water in the
fountain is the water of life.
Yes, it's true – and in the middle of it all – sits Keats
and he is become well again – with the throb and sparkle
and urgency of life. He is writing and reading, reading and
   writing. People crowd him to listen to the poems
and they bring him pizza and they bring him wine and he
writes up a storm of poems. And then
Fanny joins him, she shimmy-dances across the square,
like some silver gypsy girl – she dances
and Keats feels the poems rise up from his feet and burst
out through his soul and they dance with the gypsy girl.
And the men and women in the square sing and dance with
happiness for Keats.
'You are not just a memory,' they shout, 'you are here with
   us now…'
and the poems become silver fish that rise and dance in the
   fountain – and the golden-feathered birds make an arc
   above his head
and myself sits and marvels – like a child at his feet.
All of life bursts out like spring from the earth in Piazza
   Navona
and Keats is become well again, at the heart of it.

Watcher of the Skies

When they tell you I am gone –
do not believe them.
But rather I am simply lost in space.
I am the new planet you cannot see – there,
where the purple comet hides behind the old moon.
My coat is made of the stars and my shoes of the sun.
I hoped it would come to this.
I dreamed it would come to this.
When as a child the skies drew me in, and the gentle
orb of my soul saw I had friends – they could not
stop me watching. I would not leave.
Sometimes at night I would stand alone and breathe in
the universe, the whole of it, all its joys and sorrows.
Like a king, the night sky, and then the gentle queen of
    the dawn as the blackbird sings his heart away.
There is no poetry that can capture the sky, as the moments
    turn into green surrender to Earth's delight.
Though I will try to enslave the sky with words
I cannot succeed.
This is every poet's task – to watch the skies.
And to leave them as they found them.
Dazzling as the blackbird's song.
And free as life itself.

The Romany Ghosts of My Father

They say –
'We'll see you when we see you, but for now
let's go travelling.'

They are here again –
the Romany ghosts of my father.
Always they wonder what's out there –
what lies beyond.
The Call of the Wild Blue Yonder – the Open Road.
Things to do – places to go – people to see –
a man about a dog…
(Do you like dogs?)

They say –
'What in the name of God are you doing *inside*?
Is that any way for one of our *own* to be?
Come on, now – let's go travelling.
Hang the pots and hang the pans
and go hang all the rest –
just the feel of the sun on your back and your two hands
grappling with eternity – just think –
What May or May Not Happen
Cannot Happen in the One Place.
Life needs movement,'
say the Romany ghosts of my father.

'Alright then – pack a few things, if you must.
Pack a squirrel, and a ginnel, a soup-opener and a cat –
even a hat – but *let's* go…
Pack a song for your heart on an old handcart,
pack a mystery moment,

pack a mad March hare – if you dare – but
let's be off – before the day breaks,
before the last road calls, before the magic is gone,'
say the Romany ghosts of my father.

'Alright then, pack nothing – except laughter and long days –
and just keep walking (and spieling and talking)
and walk right out that door, feel your feet upon the Road,
   the Blessed Road.
Ah, sure – *going* – that's the thing
that keeps you warm, keeps you alive.
Be the Road – we are the Road –
the Open Road that lies ahead.
You don't need walls – ah no, you don't need anything.

Except. The stars above your head
(it has always been this way).
Moving on – a different place, a better place.
The fair's in town – no, it's the circus has come –
and we're the boys to help you ma'am…
we'll build the Big Wheel –
we'll even build the carousel –
(but tell the boss to go to hell)
we go our own way when the Road outside comes calling.'

The Romany ghosts of my father,
they will never let me be. Sometimes
it's midnight – and sometimes it's just before dawn –
and they whisper –
'Come on – will you come on now? –
while the day, and the house and the world itself are
   sleeping
let's away – while there's still time and breath in your body
and hope in your heart –
pack nothing – except your good self –

for the Road outside – listen, listen well –
she is calling. Oh yes – she is calling.'

The Green Piano

Do not count the days, but rather *live* them.
Live them as if your next breath were a shipwreck,
as if your next heartbeat was the centre of a storm.
See that the pot of dreams does not stand empty and
mend all your many wars with your many selves.
Go everywhere. Do everything.
Show a little kindness – even to yourself.
Do all of this by Wednesday and
play always a green piano in your mind.
Play it as if your life depends on it which,
by the way, it does.
Set the table and eat there with someone you love.
Walk the enchanted city and walk it well.
Do not collect time in a matchbox.
If you come to a dead end, laugh and walk on.
Eat midnight between two slices of bread.
If your cat won't sing, don't force him.
If there are only five questions in the world, never learn
    the answers.
And play always that green piano in your mind.
And know your life depends on it – so *play*.

Starting Over

We will start over again.

All of us. This is my belief, always has been.

From the bottomless pit of my daydreams, I know this to be true.

I am not a badly-worked engine, simply a car that has gone off the rails.

There will be somewhere where Hoovers and headaches and hand-me-downs and

hurricanes – have no place. They cannot get a purchase.

They slide the slippery slope to nowhere – and there is simply – peace.

A wilderness of peace. A desert of peace.

And I will no longer be a car. I will be anything I desire –

and it will change every day. And it will not matter – no, not even the small things.

There will be ginger beer flowing in the fountains.

There will be a city run by wolves who can outrun the wind. I will be a wolf

making my way down a great hill at such a speed that no-one and nothing can catch me.

There will be moonlight to eat and some left over to dance by.

And there will be such wonders to see within the gates of the city that my breath

will stop then start again for joy itself.

And there will be people I have loved on every street corner – waving and laughing

and saying – 'We tried to let you know, but it's as if you couldn't hear us, your old friends.

Our voices were lost in the green air – though we called often when we saw your need was greatest.'

Yes, they will take me by the arm – and all the time in
   between will be a shadow, a memory and
through the gates of the city I will go.
And though I'll call often – through the green air to where
   you, my love, are battling –
you also will not hear me. Though I will call all the days of
   my life – all the days of your life – until
you are come to the gates of the city and we are done with
   this shadow dance.

Notes

Here's Looking at You Kid (p. 11) – This is essentially a poem about where I grew up in York. It could be difficult sometimes, if you went to a different school in the area – much of what you do that is different doesn't always make for an easy life. The phrase 'here's looking at you, kid' is of course from *Casablanca* – a film my dad and I often watched together, and a phrase we often used between us, so it brings back very happy memories. People have said they like the fact that the sun is being kept safe in the father's pocket.

Dad's Lingo (p. 12) – This poem was part of a series of poems looking at different 'lingos' we use in our everyday lives. Because all his family came from County Mayo, Dad was incredibly proud of his Irish heritage. Sometimes my mother would say that Dad and I both spoke in Irish – meaning that, if asked whether we knew the way to somewhere, our answer might well be: 'Yes, but I wouldn't start from here!' There is a different turn of mind with all things Celtic, I feel – and I have tried to capture a suggestion of it here. A lot of Irish listeners have been kind enough to really like and endorse the poem.

The Kids with the Tree House (p. 14) – This poem was a true story, in part, about a very 'posh' area near where I lived as a kid – and an infamous visit to the glorious tree house mentioned. The house with the fancy driveway is still there; we pass it occasionally.

Hospital Lingo (p. 15) – This is another 'lingo' poem. I have had a lot of dealings on the health front over the years, and rarely write about this area of life – but thought here I would make an exception. I tried to make something light-hearted, but also that people could connect and relate to, and it does seem to do that. People can identify with elements here and seem to have a really good laugh – so, I hope you can also.

French Cat in French Window (p. 17) – This has become a bit of a party piece, and is a poem often asked for by people. I like to read in different accents – and this one is done in a mock French, Clouseau-esque accent, which I have to admit is great fun to do. This poem was written about a real cat my partner Phil and I saw in a French restaurant window in the Latin Quarter. I love Paris especially – and find the Parisians have great style and attitude, as well as being very kind. This cat seemed to develop his own voice as I wrote the poem – and I like to think of him as still there, running his restaurant in the Bois de Boulogne. Maybe, one day, he'll let me have a table…

The Serving Girl (p. 18) – This poem is dedicated to my grandmother, Margaret Mack, who was brought up in Bootle, Liverpool. She travelled round Britain with her brothers who worked as navvies, and she also worked as a serving girl in local houses. (My mother later followed in this manner and went into service in London, in Chelsea – so in a way this poem is about both of them.) It won a Commended prize in the 2014 Ware Poetry Competition. She was a very strong woman by all accounts and I wish I had known her. My mother looked after her when she was very ill and always said she heard angels singing as she climbed the stairs to her room to find she had died.

The Old Pig (p. 20) – This poem won the Torbay Open Poetry Prize in 2013. It is a true story my mother told of an old pig that she looked after on the family farm in Doncaster. She told the story many times to me, and she would have been so proud to hear this poem won a prize. When I read it, I can hear her voice telling me the story – and briefly she is back with me.

My Wild Mother (p. 23) – The photo alongside this poem is me and Mam at Bray Head outside of Dublin, on our first trip to Ireland, 1962. This poem was written mostly after my mum had died, although I think she saw an early draft of it. I like to think bits of it would have made her laugh – although she would probably have been scandalised by other parts of it! I was very pleased for it to be included in the *Iron Anthology of Humorous Verse*, up in Newcastle. I have had a lot of requests for copies of this poem as people often come up and say – 'Yes! That's my mother!' So it seems there are a lot of wild and rebellious mothers out there. Just as well…

The Kindness Medal (p. 25) – This poem goes in tandem with the 'Wild Mother' poem, as I think my mum was always innately kind to people. As is the way with kindness, it doesn't seem to get much of a reward in life. The medal I show when reading this poem is a medal Mum got in Rome to commemorate the opening of the Holy Door in 1950. I have had many comments from people about this poem – it seems to really strike an emotional chord for them. Perhaps we are all aware of the kindness we meet in life – and want to sing its praises?

The Christmas Letter (p. 26) – This poem won the Waterstones Poetry Prize, and also on one occasion was part of the winning poems I read at Ilkley Literature Festival. It began life in response to a letter we receive every Christmas, a round-robin letter, and also because so many people were now sending huge Christmas missives with their cards. Gervase Phinn especially likes this poem – and I have had to send many people copies of it at different times.

Eight o'clock in Britain (p. 28) – This poem was published on a Hollywood blogzine site (the nearest I've got to Hollywood so far!) and is really a tongue-in-cheek piece about how Britain seems to shut down somewhat earlier than cities in Europe. I like the longer days and evenings that Europe creates, and wish more of that would happen here. That feeling of having more time, and the possibility to do what you want in it – that would be good!

All You Need is Love (p. 30) – I find a lot of the Beatles' lyrics very inspirational, and this poem came out of that enjoyment. Poets always write about love in one way or another, so it was tricky to try and find a new angle. I think listening to sixties music helped – and this poem has its own particular rhythm. People seem to enjoy its diversity and approach, and I hope one day to read it at the Casbah Club, where the Beatles first played, in Liverpool. I just visited there for my birthday and touched the lucky dragon on the wall.

Sixties Anthem (p. 33) – This poem goes with the previous one, of course. It incorporates a lot of ridiculous things I did in the sixties. That feeling of 'anything goes' – and of being in the moment, just being alive – is what I wanted to capture here. I have taken a bit of poetic licence with some of the facts!

Baxter's Crime (p. 34) – This poem was published in a micro-chapbook in America by Origami Poems. It was written about a real dog that seemed to be walked regularly down the back street behind my house. I heard him every day, though never saw him, so he became a distant friend. People often seem to identify with Baxter, as described in the poem – and I know I do. He has now had several illustrations done of him as well. I think he will feature in a story eventually.

The Kindness of Dogs (p. 36) – I often seem to write poems about dogs. Like birds, they represent freedom and playfulness to me. A phrase of my dad's was 'I'm not bad for a two-year-old dog...' and I concur with this. The kind nature of dogs is what I hoped to capture here – and if you have a dog yourself, I hope you like it.

Distance (p. 38) – This poem was written shortly after my dad had died. I still miss his extraordinary sense of humour and storytelling ability, which was remarkable. I remember he told me he would 'hang on' for as long as he could, but when he was gone, he would still be thinking of me. He said there is a light that shines for me, in the darkness – and that I was not to be sad. I hope he would have liked this poem, and what I try to achieve through all of the poems. The stories we write with our hearts are what matter.

A wheelchair goes into a bar (p. 39) – This poem is about my travels in a wheelchair over the last four or five years. A lot of the anecdotes are based on fact, and although I don't write about this subject very much, here I thought I had found a way for the subject to still be entertaining as well as making people think.

The Open Door (p. 41) – This poem was written one day when I really wanted to get out of the house, and due to health issues, couldn't. Birds often feature in my work, as I love the freedom they represent. Keeping doors open, both literally and in the mind, is what keeps a writer alive I think. When people get this poem they really 'get' it – and I would like to think it's a stepping stone for someone moving through a not-so-great moment, heading towards a more hopeful one.

The Lucky Dip Machine of the Magic Bird of Fortune (p. 42) – This poem was written four or five years ago, and has never been published anywhere previously. It has, however, become a firm favourite for people to read at times of romantic celebration. I believe it has been greatly enjoyed at weddings, recently – and my partner Phil was the inspiration for it.

My Mother, the Mustang (p. 44) – I love images of wild horses and often draw them. With their tremendous independence, mystery and wildness, they seem to represent the very essence of my mother, who was a woman of great strength and character – but who also was always impossible to fully describe. A delightful enigma!

What They Found in the Poet's Stomach (p. 46) – This poem, and the next, were written in 2014 especially for the Keats-Shelley House in Rome. I have based this first one not only on the very short but brilliant life of Keats, but also what it is about poetry that draws us in to write in this way. No-one chooses to be a poet, I think, and quite often we stand upon the shoulders of poets who have gone before us.

Keats in Piazza Navona (p. 47) – Piazza Navona is one of my favourite squares in Rome, as it is a great people-watching arena. I imagine Keats coming back to life there, and enjoying all that Roman life has to offer – the vibrancy, the colour, the beauty.

Watcher of the Skies (p. 48) – I was privileged this year to be asked to judge the Keats-Shelley House Poetry Prize for Children and Young People, and this poem was written to perform for the bicentenary of Keats. When he was a youngster and in his school playground, Keats was very fond of watching the skies, turning round and round to do so. He had a keen interest in the sky and I hope he might have liked this poem.

The Romany Ghosts of My Father (p. 49) – This poem is a particular favourite of mine as it relates specifically to my dad's family, who all came across from County Mayo. They were a big Catholic family and mainly settled in the Walmgate district of York – which was really a little Ireland. Some eventually emigrated to New York and Boston, while others settled more locally in Leeds. The poem came to me all of a piece, and was like a refrain in my head for some days. It has often been performed to music, and I would like to perform it one day in Mayo. Am writing this on Dad's birthday – so – here's looking at you, Dad!

The Green Piano (p. 53) – This poem has never been published before, and it is the poem I am asked for most. People always want a copy of it – I have read it at literary events, folk festivals and cabarets, and it seems to appeal to all ages and all backgrounds of people. It's about living every moment of your life just as it comes and *to the full*. It was written all of a single piece, sitting in my conservatory one sunny afternoon.

Starting Over (p. 54) – This poem is for my partner Phil, without whom very few of these poems would have been written – he is my 'Bridge Over Troubled Water'. He is what makes the day complete and allows me to continue to tinker at the green piano of poetry that is always playing in my mind. Here's looking at you, kid – here's looking at you.